RED ARROWS

The Red Arrows have performed more than 5,000 displays worldwide since their formation in 1965.

RED ARROWS

HIGH FLYERS

CAROLINE "BLAZE" JENSEN

CREATIVE EDUCATION · CREATIVE PAPERBACKS

Published by Creative Education and Creative Paperbacks
P.O. Box 227, Mankato, Minnesota 56002
Creative Education and Creative Paperbacks are imprints of The Creative Company
www.thecreativecompany.us

Book Design by Wyeth Morgan
Art direction by Blue Design (www.bluedes.com)

Images by Associated Press/Gareth Fuller, cover; Getty Images/Danny Lawson - PA Images, 1, 32, Richard Baker, 27; Pexels/Kimberley Madigan, 11; Public Domain/United Kingdom Ministry of Defense, 7, 12–13, 18, 28; Wikimedia Commons/Arpingstone, 22, B. Huber, 16, Cpl. Andy Benson, 8, Cpl Phil Dye, 4–5, H. D. Girdwood, 14, Julian Herzog, 25, Nick, 21, Ronnie Macdonald, 10, SAC Craig Marshall (RAF)/MOD, 26, SAC Tim Laurence, 6, Sgt Ashley Keates/MOD, 30, Tony Hisgett, 2

Library of Congress Cataloging-in-Publication Data
Names: Jensen, Caroline, author.
Title: Red Arrows / Caroline "Blaze" Jensen.
Description: Mankato, Minnesota : Creative Education and Creative Paperbacks, [2026] | Series: High flyers | Includes bibliographical references and index. | Audience: Ages 10-13 | Audience: Grades 4-6 | Summary: "Diamond nines. Rollbacks. Corkscrews. The British Royal Air Force Red Arrows perform stunning aerobatic displays. Soar high with the Red Arrows in this visually stunning introduction to their history, present, and future, geared toward upper-elementary readers"— Provided by publisher.
Identifiers: LCCN 2025015366 (print) | LCCN 2025015367 (ebook) | ISBN 9798895810644 (library binding) | ISBN 9798896800170 (paperback) | ISBN 9798895811900 (ebook)
Subjects: LCSH: Great Britain. Royal Air Force. Aerobatic team--Juvenile literature. | Stunt flying--Great Britain—Juvenile literature. | Aeronautics, Military—Great Britain—Juvenile literature. | Air shows—Great Britain—Juvenile literature. | CYAC: Stunt flying. | Military aeronautics. | Air shows.
Classification: LCC UG632.3.G7 J46 2026 (print) | LCC UG632.3.G7 (ebook) | DDC 797.5/40941—dc23/eng/20250512
LC record available at https://lccn.loc.gov/2025015366
LC ebook record available at https://lccn.loc.gov/2025015367

Printed in the United States

ABOUT THE AUTHOR — **Caroline "Blaze" Jensen flew 3,600 hours in the Air Force as a fighter pilot, including F-16 combat missions and Thunderbirds demonstrations. She lives in Wisconsin with her son, Finn, and dog, Gunner. She loves sharing her passion for flying with kids of all ages.**

The Red Arrows fly the BAe Hawk T.1.

CONTENTS

WING TIPS

The Red Arrows started with seven jets, increasing to nine in 1968. ➘

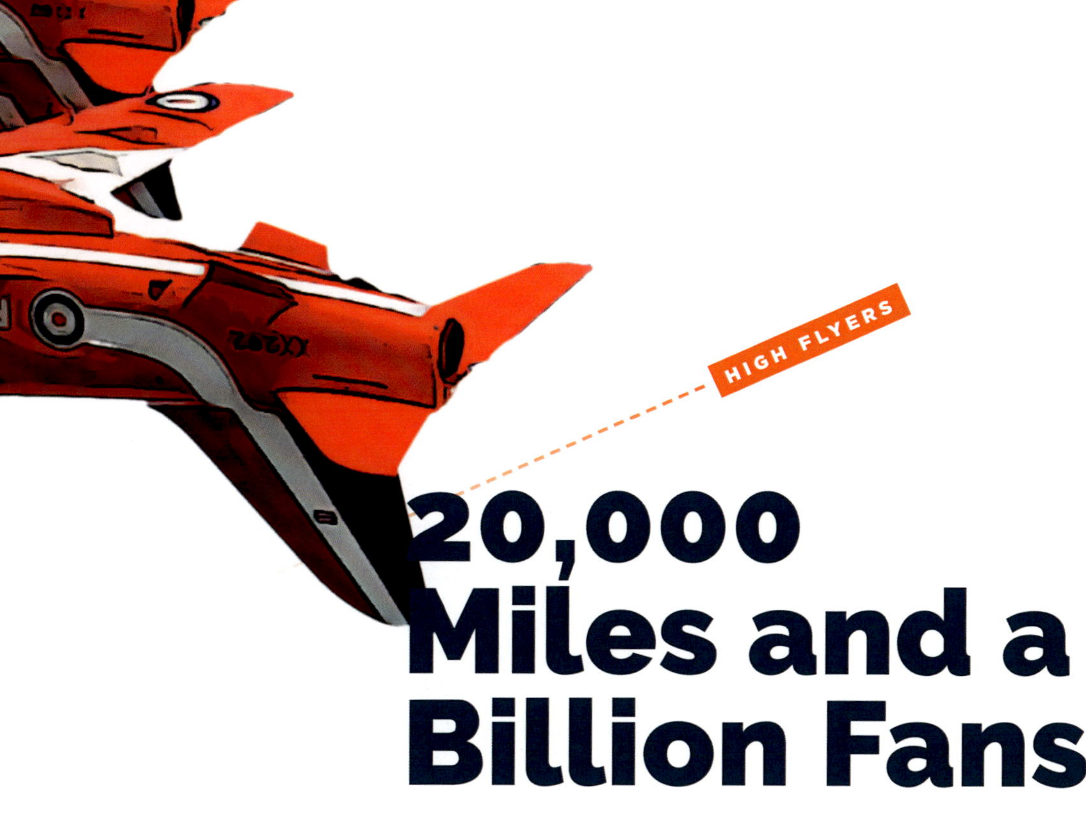

HIGH FLYERS

20,000 Miles and a Billion Fans

The crowd stared in awe as nine red jets, trailing blue, white, and red smoke, streaked across the sky in their famous diamond nine formation. The Royal Air Force (RAF) air display team, the Red Arrows, was in China for the first time.

In November 2016, the Red Arrows performed nine times in six days in China. On their nine-week trip to the Asia-Pacific and Middle East regions, they covered 20,000 miles (32,187 kilometers) and visited 17 countries. About one billion fans watched their shows in person and online.

The Red Arrows are one of the oldest and most famous aerobatic teams in the world. They started more than one hundred years ago and are known for their flying skills and stunning displays. Their mission is to show British fighter pilots' talent and inspire people, especially young kids, to get interested in flying.

THE DYE GUYS

Two teams of engineers travel with the pilots. They make sure the Red Arrows have their pods of colored dyes ready for each show. The pods are stored under the main body of the jet. The dyes are sprayed into the hot exhaust from the jet engines, creating blue, white, and red trails of smoke in the sky. These are the colors of the British flag. The colorful smoke makes the formations and stunts easier to see and more exciting.

Each jet carries enough dye for five minutes of white smoke and one minute of red and blue smoke.

The colorful displays created by the Red Arrows thrill people around the world.

The British military used airplanes to patrol over German lines.

From Biplanes to Jet Planes

During World War I (1914–18), the British Army and Navy had their own small air forces, but they didn't work together well. Airplanes were very useful in the war, flying over enemy lines to gather information. By the end of the war, the British government decided to create a separate air force just for flying, and the RAF was born in 1918. British airshows became an important part of the country's aviation culture, displaying both military and civilian pilot skills.

Spitfire MKI

After the war, airshows celebrated advances in aviation and demonstrated the increasing abilities of the air forces. The first major airshow was the London Airshow in 1920 at the Hendon Aerodrome. It attracted large crowds and featured new aircraft displays.

The Royal Air Force Display, started in the 1920s, was one of the earliest airshows. The planes performed simple aerobatics and formation flying to interest the public in aviation. In the 1930s, as tensions grew in Europe leading to World War II (1939–45), airshows featuring the Hawker Fury aircraft showcased the RAF's capabilities.

Aerobatics became more difficult as biplanes gave way to jet aircraft. Jets turned and flew much faster. When the RAF switched to flying jets, it needed a new kind of pilot. It wanted the airshows to not just entertain but also inspire kids to become pilots someday.

Different RAF flying units had their own teams. One famous team, the Black Arrows, flew de Havilland Vampire and Hawker Hunter jets. They performed loops and rolls with multiple planes, laying the groundwork for future aerobatic teams.

'NEVER WAS SO MUCH OWED BY SO MANY TO SO FEW'

British Prime Minister Winston Churchill spoke these famous words after the Battle of Britain during World War II. British people living under the air battles could look up and see the fighter pilots defending their country against the German Luftwaffe (Air Force). The combat was often so low that people could see dogfights with their own eyes. Civilians created the Royal Observer Corps to track, identify, and warn their country's defenders of incoming enemy planes.

Airshows were exciting but also dangerous. In 1952, a de Havilland Comet 1 passenger plane crashed at the Farnborough Airshow. When test pilot John Derry flew a steep climb and took a sharp turn to show off the speed and maneuverability of the passenger craft, the plane broke apart and fell to the ground. Three crew members, including the pilot, were killed. Several people on the ground were killed or hurt by pieces of the plane falling from the sky. The accident scared many people and led to improvements in aviation safety, including better safety procedures, aircraft design, and pilot training.

Other teams had unique names like the Yellow Jackets and the Red Pelicans. The most famous team before the Red Arrows was the Blue Diamonds, formed in 1960. They flew the English Electric Lightning aircraft and were one of the first teams to perform high-speed aerobatic displays. In 1964, the Blue Diamonds were disbanded. The newly formed Red Arrows took on their role, continuing to perform today.

GUINNESS BOOK OF WORLD RECORDS

In 1958, the Black Arrows, a British aerobatic team, set a world record by performing an amazing stunt called the "the 22-jet loop." They flew 22 planes in close formation through a perfect loop in the sky. It was the largest formation of planes to ever do a loop and set a world record. That world record has never been broken. It became one of the most famous moments in British aviation history.

The Red Arrows Are Official

The Red Arrows have flown only two types of aircraft since they were founded in 1964. The first was the Folland Gnat T.1, a small, lightweight jet chosen for its ease of handling and suitability for aerobatic stunts. The Gnat was fast and maneuverable. The Red Arrows used it for 15 years before switching to a new aircraft.

Since 1979, the Red Arrows have flown the BAe Hawk T.1, a more modern jet capable of higher speeds and more complex aerobatic maneuvers. The Hawk is small, light, and very maneuverable. It can be used as a trainer, to fight other airplanes, or to bomb targets on the ground. The Red Arrows added colorful smoke to make their performances even more exciting.

The Red Arrows squadron has 16 airplanes in total and travels with 10 aircraft to each show. Nine aircraft perform, and one is a spare. The nine positions on the team are numbered from 1 to 9, with the 10th being the narrator's plane. Red 1 is the leader, responsible for guiding the team, making decisions, and keeping everyone safe. Red 2 is the left wing, flying just to the left of Red 1. This position requires excellent flying skills to maintain perfect distance and angles in tight formations. Red 3 is to the right of Red 1, working with Red 2 to keep formations perfectly aligned. Red 4 and 5 are the second left and right wings, flying off Red 2 and 3. They help to keep the team balanced and work with the other pilots to create symmetrical patterns. Red 6 flies right behind the leader in "close formation." Red 7 and 8 are "opposition" pilots, flying towards or around the rest of the team to create exciting patterns. Red 9, the "tail end Charlie," ensures the team looks perfect from the back. The jets rely on engineers, the mechanics for the planes.

The support team members are called "the Blues," and the team that travels with the Red Arrows to shows is called "the Circus." Being part of such a hard-working team means getting along well with teammates.

The team does not use the RAF's newest fighter jets but older trainers. They take good care of their trainers, but the planes will eventually need repairs. Soon, there may not be enough parts left for the aircraft, so the Red Arrows will likely be performing in new aircraft.

FARNBOROUGH AIRSHOW

The Farnborough Airshow is one of the most famous airshows in the world. It is held in Farnborough, England. It started in 1948 and has been held every two years since. At this show, amazing planes, both military and civilian, are flown for the crowds. It is where new aircraft and technology are shown, and pilots perform daring stunts. People from all over the world come to see the latest in aviation and watch the performances. Jet teams from other countries, like the Patrouille de France from France and the Frecce Tricolori from Italy, often participate, too.

The Red Arrows are very careful in choosing the best pilots.

Team Selection and Training

The mission of the Red Arrows is to recruit more pilots for the RAF. Many pilots remember wanting to fly for the team since they were as young as five years old. Each year, about 50 pilots apply for this special assignment, often applying multiple times before being selected. They must have at least 1,500 flying hours and be considered above-average pilots. They spend about three years training and then have two more regular tours of military duty before joining the team. The Red

Arrows usually start with 50 applicants, narrow them down to 9, and select the best 3 to fly for the team. The selection process takes about five years from the first application to being hired.

The home of the Red Arrows is RAF Waddington, but they also train at other locations to prepare for the new season. Training in several locations allows the team to fly over various types of land and deal with different weather challenges.

Three pilots leave the team each year, and three new pilots join to achieve their dream of becoming a Red Arrow. The training is intense, with six 30-minute practices scheduled. Initially, the pilots fly with two or three other aircraft at a

FLY TIGHT

The Red Arrows rely on clear and fast communication to perform safely. They use radios to stay tight and know what is coming up next. They also use hand signals to communicate without speaking. The formation leader makes radio calls that the other pilots can hear, telling them what to do and when to do it. Radio calls might include "smoke on, ready now," "box formation go," or "pulling up now." Each pilot must listen carefully and respond quickly to ensure everyone stays safe while performing tricky maneuvers.

The planes are perfectly lined up when they fly.

higher altitude. They gradually add more aircraft and lower their minimum altitude until they can safely perform the whole show.

Strict planning and preparation are key to the team's safety. Before each training session or official display, the Red Arrows spend a lot of time planning. They go over each maneuver in detail, considering the weather, airspace needed, and how to avoid bad situations. Experienced pilots also do safety drills and checks. Each

A Red Arrows pilot is greeted by his son after returning to home base.

aircraft is thoroughly checked to ensure it's in perfect condition. The Red Arrows can fly very close together and use a special radio to communicate, helping them stay aware of each other's movements to avoid accidents.

The support team, known as "the Blues," represents various professions from across the RAF. During the training season, all pilots and crew wear green uniforms. After completing training and being cleared to represent the RAF, the pilots wear red flight suits, and the ground crew wears blue flight suits. Major maintenance is done during the winter training season to ensure the jets are ready for the demanding show season.

↗ A support team, dressed in blue, helps maintain the Red Arrows' airplanes.

The Red Arrows perform for more than a million fans every summer.

Thrilling Maneuvers

Being a Red Arrow means striving to be the best. The Red Arrows are the United Kingdom's ambassadors to the world, giving about 100 shows each summer for more than a million fans. The whole show is spectacular, but some maneuvers are crowd favorites.

The Heart is one of the most romantic and beautiful maneuvers. As the name suggests, it creates a heart in the sky. The Red Arrows fly in a wide formation, looping and twisting to form a perfect heart. The maneuver is stunning to watch, especially when the planes leave behind their colorful smoke trails. It is a

The Red Arrows perform a joint show with the U.S. Air Force Thunderbirds.

SPECIAL PASS-BYS

The Red Arrows often do special pass-by flights at events to add excitement and honor important occasions. A pass-by is when the team flies over an area in a tight formation, usually at a low altitude, so everyone can see them. They sometimes fly over big events like football (soccer) matches, parades, or celebrations. It's a great way for the team to show their skills and make a big moment even more memorable.

favorite for Valentine's Day airshows or other special occasions. It's a beautiful and graceful way to show off the Red Arrows' creativity and precision.

The Split is a maneuver where the Red Arrows start in a tight formation and then suddenly break into two groups. One group flies straight ahead while the other turns sharply to the side. It looks like the team is splitting in two, but it's all part of the plan! The two groups often cross paths in the air, performing loops and rolls. The Split shows how well the pilots control their planes and react to each other's movements. It's fast, dramatic, and often sets up other stunts.

Since the team has been flying the BAe Hawk T.1 for over 40 years, they may need to switch to a new plane soon. The Hawk is harder to find parts for due to its age. If the Red Arrows switch planes, it will be a big change, but they will continue to perform stunning shows for fans worldwide.

The Red Arrows have flown nearly 5,000 shows in 57 countries, including China, India, the United States, Canada, and other countries in the Middle East and Asia-Pacific regions. However, the pilots say some of their favorite airshows are the ones they perform in front of their hometowns.

The next time you see a Red Arrows performance, remember it's not just about the planes. It's the amazing pilots and their teamwork that make the magical stunts happen.

INDEX